# SHAYS' REBELLION

BY BLAKE HOENA
ILLUSTRATED BY EDUARDO GARCIA

CONSULTANT:
JAMES DIMOCK
PROFESSOR OF COMMUNICATION STUDIES
MINNESOTA STATE UNIVERSITY, MANKATO

CAPSTONE PRESS
a capstone imprint

Published by Capstone Press, an imprint of Capstone.
1710 Roe Crest Drive, North Mankato, Minnesota 56003
capstonepub.com

Library of Congress Cataloging-in-Publication Data
Names: Hoena, B. A., author. I Garcia, Eduardo, 1970 August 31– illustrator.
Title: Shays' Rebellion / by Blake Hoena ; illustrated by Eduardo Garcia.
Description: North Mankato, Minnesota : Capstone Press, [2022] I Series: Movements and resistance I Includes bibliographical references. I Audience: Ages 8–11 I Audience: Grades 4–6 I Summary: "In 1786, the Massachusetts government was seizing farmers' lands and throwing the farmers in jail for unpaid debts and taxes. But many people couldn't pay because they had not yet been paid for fighting in the Revolutionary War just a few years before. Frustrated by this treatment, Daniel Shays led upset citizens in an armed revolt. Although their rebellion was short lived, it made clear to America's leaders that the young nation needed to change its laws, paving the way for the creation of the U.S. Constitution"—Provided by publisher.
Identifiers: LCCN 2021030702 (print) I LCCN 2021030703 (ebook) I ISBN 9781663959249 (hardcover) I ISBN 9781666323016 (paperback) I ISBN 9781666323009 (pdf) I ISBN 9781666323054 (kindle edition)
Subjects: LCSH: Shays' Rebellion, 1786–1787—Juvenile literature. I Shays' Rebellion, 1786–1787—Comic books, strips, etc. I LCGFT: Graphic novels.
Classification: LCC F69 .H64 2022 (print) I LCC F69 (ebook) I DDC 974.4/03—dc23
LC record available at https://lccn.loc.gov/2021030702
LC ebook record available at https://lccn.loc.gov/2021030703

Editorial Credits
Editor: Christopher Harbo; Designer: Tracy Davies;
Media Researcher: Svetlana Zhurkin; Production Specialist: Katy LaVigne

The illustrator would like to thank his son, Sebastian Garcia,
for his help with the art in this book.

All internet sites appearing in back matter were available
and accurate when this book was sent to press.

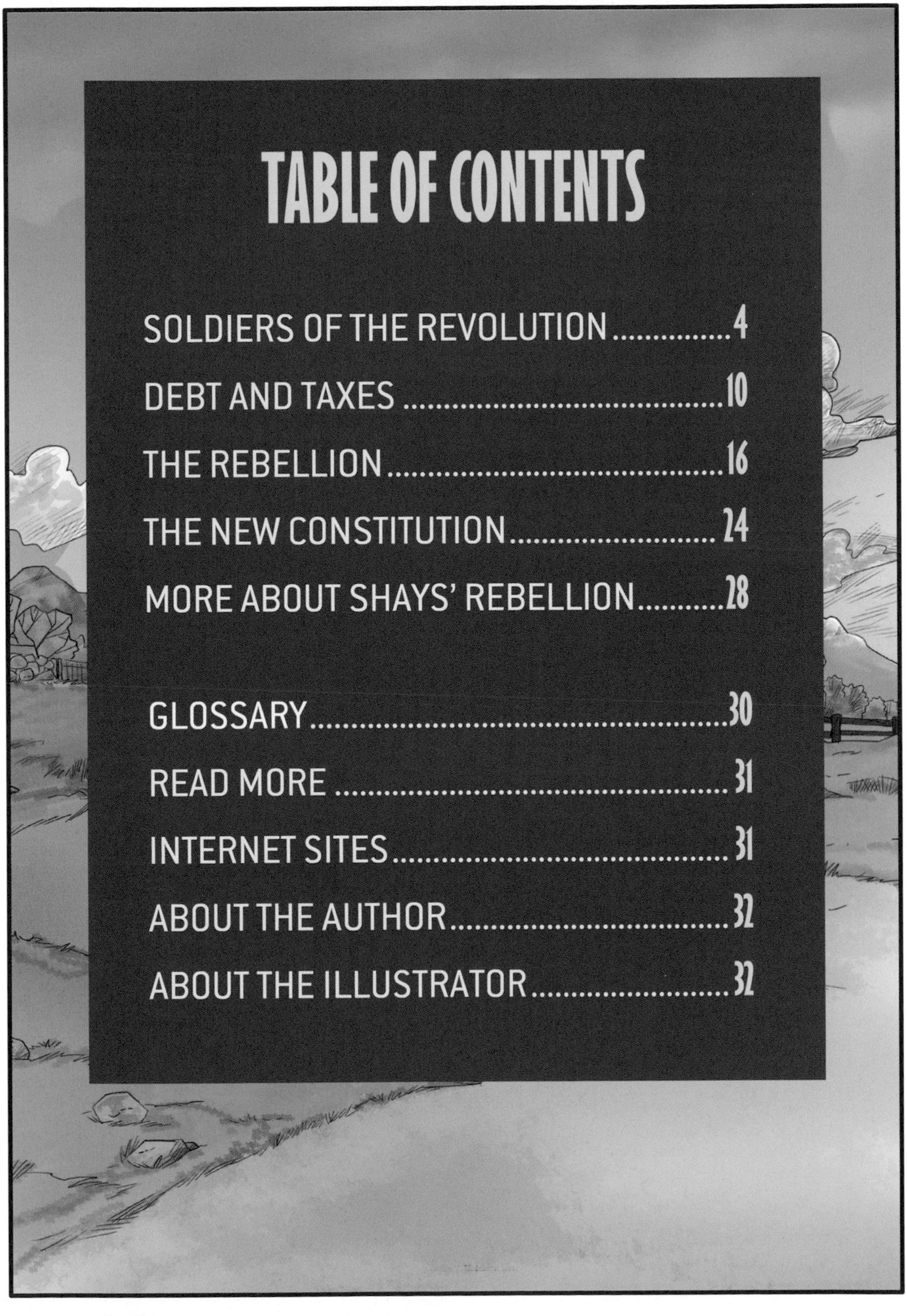

# TABLE OF CONTENTS

# SOLDIERS OF THE REVOLUTION

On April 19, 1775, when the "shot heard round the world" rang out, Daniel Shays was there. At the time, he was just a poor farmer living in Massachusetts. But he took up arms along with hundreds of minutemen. They prepared to face the British in a battle that would ignite the war for American independence.

Come on, Shays, the British are on the march to Concord!

The Colonists won the Battles of Lexington and Concord, but they were in for a long, hard-fought war. The British redcoats were professional soldiers. They were highly trained and well-equipped. The Colonial army was made up mostly of men like Shays, who often had to supply their own muskets and uniforms.

Go back to Boston, redcoats!

RETREAT!

When off fighting, these men could not tend to their crops or work their jobs. Many had to rely on what they earned as soldiers to support their families.

Sergeant Daniel Shays, 18 shillings, 10 pence, for your last eleven days of service.

Not long after the first shots were fired, the Second Continental Congress met. This group of lawmakers from the 13 colonies would be in charge of the war effort.

CLAP!

CLAP!

CLAP!

It has been decided. George Washington of Virginia will lead the Continental Army.

During the early years of the war, Congress approved two important documents. In July 1776, its members approved the Declaration of Independence, which united the colonies against Great Britain.

... these United Colonies are, and of Right ought to be Free and Independent States ...

In November 1777, its members approved the Articles of Confederation, the first constitution of the United States of America. It gave Congress power to govern the new nation, yet it did not give Congress the ability to collect taxes.

Only the states should have the right to tax their citizens!

And without a way to raise money, Congress struggled to pay soldiers of the Continental Army.

Sorry, Shays. This month's pay has been delayed.

I'll need to borrow more money to send home.

What, no pay again?

I need new boots. How am I supposed to pay for them?

Even so, Shays continued to fight bravely for America's freedom. He rose to the rank of captain.

Quiet, men. We don't want the British to know we're here.

He was even honored by Marquis de Lafayette, the French general who famously fought alongside General Washington.

In recognition of your courage and loyalty to your country, I present you with this ceremonial sword.

In spite of all he had done, Shays struggled financially like many other soldiers.

Your fellow officers will frown upon you for selling this sword.

I have no other choice if I am to pay my debts.

In 1780, Shays retired from the army and returned to his farm in Massachusetts.

Did you receive the back pay you are owed for your years of service?

Hardly a cent of it, Abigail.

What of our debts?

Perhaps I can sell off some land . . .

While Shays left the army, other soldiers continued to serve under poor conditions.

Wish I had a decent pair of boots. My toes are frostbit.

There's hardly anything to eat except stale bread.

And we haven't been paid in nearly a year!

On January 1, 1781, a group of 1,500 disgruntled soldiers from Pennsylvania decided they'd had enough. They revolted against their commanders in what is known as the Mutiny of the Pennsylvania Line.

Stop this mutiny—

Grab him, men!

ugh!

Then the soldiers marched toward Philadelphia, where the Continental Congress was in session.

If our commanders won't listen to us, we'll take our complaints to Congress!

General George Washington heard about the revolt. He quickly wrote letters to several state governors, asking for financial help.

. . . furnish at least three months' pay for the troops, which will be of some value to them, and at the same time ways and means are devised to clothe and feed them better.

Congress sent an emissary to negotiate with the soldiers.

I've been sent here to address your grievances.

The rebellion ended peacefully once many of the soldiers were allowed to leave the army. But this was not the only time soldiers revolted due to lack of pay and poor conditions.

# DEBT AND TAXES

While the new nation struggled to hold its army together, soldiers of the Continental Army continued to fight on. Then, in the fall of 1781, the final battle of the Revolutionary War was fought at Yorktown, Virginia.

I offer you General Cornwallis' sword in surrender.

It ended with British General Cornwallis surrendering to General George Washington. A peace treaty was signed two years later, bringing an official close to the war.

George Washington resigned as commander of the Continental Army and returned home.

After all these years, it's good to have you home again.

With my time in public life over, Martha, I'll be happy to spend my days here with you in Mount Vernon.

With independence won, many expected their lives to improve. Poor farmers and enslaved people had also dreamed of a nation of freedom and prosperity for all. This is why the Revolutionary War was fought. While some were forced to keep silent, Shays often heard soldiers complain at Conkey's Tavern.

Greetings, Mr. Shays.

Greetings, to you. How have you been faring since the war?

Times are tough.

States like Massachusetts had fallen into debt because of the costly war. To pay their debts, they taxed their citizens.

If I don't receive back pay from the military soon, I'll be summoned to debtor's court.

And what were we fighting for anyway? We pay more taxes now than we did under British rule.

And no one is speaking up for farmers like us!

On January 5, 1782, former minister Samuel Ely spoke of a growing resentment spreading throughout Massachusetts.

Government officials have been corrupted by too much power and too much wealth, and for that, they don't deserve our respect!

No more taxes!

Liberty for the common folk!

One major problem of the time was the lack of money. In Massachusetts, members of the state legislature did not want paper money used to pay for goods and services.

We request the printing of paper money, so that farmers have a way of paying their taxes and debts.

But a flood of paper money will drive up the cost of goods and ruin the economy.

That meant people were forced to barter for goods and services, or use hard currency, such as gold and silver. But hard currency was very difficult to come by.

Your taxes have come due.

I would pay, if there was money to pay with.

To make matters worse, the state government continued to impose new taxes.

The price of newspapers has gone up with the new stamp tax.

Stamp tax? Like the British Stamp Act that helped cause the revolution?

And then in 1785, James Bowdoin became governor of Massachusetts. Though soldiers still had not received pay for their service during the war, he called for stricter enforcement of tax collections.

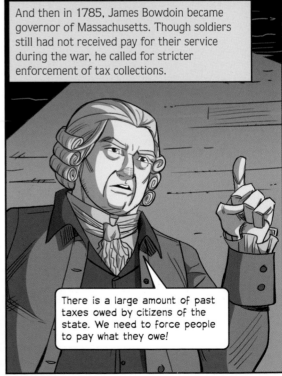

There is a large amount of past taxes owed by citizens of the state. We need to force people to pay what they owe!

If a person could not pay, they could lose their property . . .

You have failed to pay taxes owed. Therefore, your farm will be put up for auction.

. . . be thrown in debtors' prison . . .

. . . or be forced to work to pay off their debts.

In late August 1786, community leaders asked that debt relief be given to farmers suffering under the weight of high taxes. The Massachusetts state legislature refused this request. Angry citizens, known as Regulators, then took up arms in protest.

Where are the judges?

They will hear our demands!

Several hundred Regulators marched on the courthouse in Northampton, Massachusetts. They wanted to prevent judges from hearing cases against people who had unpaid taxes.

I doubt court will be held today. I'd better get you to safety.

Quick, get inside.

We will not leave until our concerns about the lack of money and these outrageous taxes are resolved.

They wanted to keep people from being prosecuted because of their debts.

Then we have no choice but to adjourn this quarterly court session.

14

Job Shattuck became one of the leaders of the Regulators. Like Shays, he was a veteran of the Revolutionary War. He had also risen to the rank of captain.

Head over to the green. We'll set up camp near the courthouse.

In early September 1786, he returned to Concord as the head of a large group of Regulators.

Hard to believe I'm back here preparing for another battle.

Like in Northampton, Shattuck also blocked judges from entering the courthouse.

This letter states that we will not allow you to hear any cases until the people are heard and their grievances addressed.

# THE REBELLION

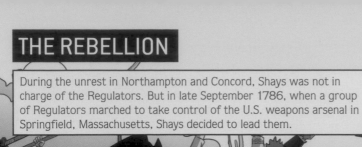

During the unrest in Northampton and Concord, Shays was not in charge of the Regulators. But in late September 1786, when a group of Regulators marched to take control of the U.S. weapons arsenal in Springfield, Massachusetts, Shays decided to lead them.

I better take command of this group, or there could be bloodshed.

March on the courthouse!

They will hear our demands!

Force them to close the courts!

This time the state militia was prepared to defend the courthouse, with General William Shepard leading them.

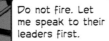

Do not fire. Let me speak to their leaders first.

We do not want a fight. Our intent is only to march to the courthouse so that our demands are heard.

I will allow it as long as no one causes trouble.

The situation was tense. But thanks to Shays' leadership, everything remained peaceful and the Regulators achieved their goal of shutting down the courthouse.

Tell the judges that we will not allow them to proceed with any cases involving unpaid debts or taxes.

The actions of the Regulators angered Governor Bowdoin.

We must take extreme measures to restore the dignity of the government. If that means raising an army, so be it! Even if it means arresting the leaders of these insurgents, that's what we must do!

Shays expected the state government to react harshly. So he sent a letter to the leaders of the Regulators to be prepared.

I request you to assemble your men together, to see that they are all armed and equipped with sixty rounds, each man to be ready to turn out at a minute's warning.

Then on November 29, 1786, Job Shattuck was arrested.

Did you hear the news about Shattuck?

The seeds of war are now sown.

Early in December, the Regulators began to organize themselves into a more military-like force. They also shut down several courts meeting in December and early January.

Shays, you'll captain the fourth regiment out of Pelham.

Where will we march next?

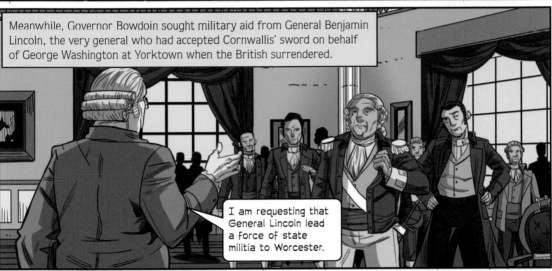

Meanwhile, Governor Bowdoin sought military aid from General Benjamin Lincoln, the very general who had accepted Cornwallis' sword on behalf of George Washington at Yorktown when the British surrendered.

I am requesting that General Lincoln lead a force of state militia to Worcester.

The next court session was to be held there on January 23, 1787.

It's a three-day march, men, and we want to arrive in Worcester before the rebels.

Shays and the Regulators had planned to march on Worcester, but . . .

General Lincoln has 3,000 soldiers with him.

That's too large of a force for us to face.

Perhaps we should march on Springfield instead. We could raid the arsenal, and then we'd be better prepared to take on General Lincoln.

Meanwhile, General Shepard was preparing for a possible attack. He had a force of about 1,200 militiamen with him at the arsenal in Springfield.

We best be ready in case the mob marches our way.

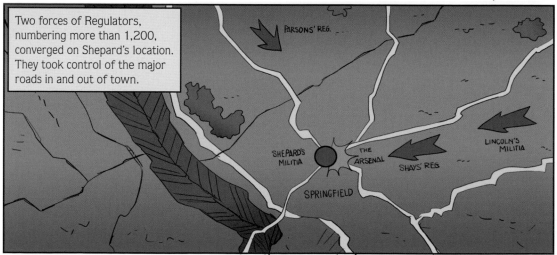

Two forces of Regulators, numbering more than 1,200, converged on Shepard's location. They took control of the major roads in and out of town.

PARSONS' REG.

SHEPARD'S MILITIA

THE ARSENAL

SHAYS' REG.

LINCOLN'S MILITIA

SPRINGFIELD

Then on January 25, Shays' forces made their move.

Onward, men!

Fire a warning shot over their heads!

BOOM!

CRASH!

But Shays' men kept marching forward.

Keep marching, men!

Then, when Shays' men were about 100 feet away . . .

Fire upon them!

BOOM!

AHHH!

UGH

Shays tried to rally his men . . .

Return fire! RETURN FIRE!

. . . but the Regulators were defeated without firing a shot. Three men were killed during the brief battle, and one would die later from his wounds. Several others were injured.

General Lincoln pursued the remaining Regulator forces to the town of Petersham. Most of them were captured on February 4, 1787.

Surrender, and your lives will be spared.

Several other Regulators, including Shays, fled to the state of Vermont. People there were also suffering from high taxes and unpaid debts and were supportive of the Regulators' cause.

In the end, most of the Regulators who marched into battle with Shays received a pardon. Even Shays, after swearing a renewed loyalty to the government, would eventually receive a pardon on June 25, 1788. But he would never return to his home in Massachusetts.

By the spring of 1787, Shays' Rebellion had ended. But the actions of the Regulators deeply divided the nation. Some of the nation's founders, such as Thomas Jefferson, saw their cause as just . . .

I hold it that a little rebellion now and then is a good thing. . . . It is a medicine necessary for the sound health of government.

. . . while others, like Samuel Adams, saw it as treasonous.

The man who dares to rebel against the laws of a republic ought to suffer death.

But most lawmakers agreed that the rebellion also highlighted flaws in the Articles of Confederation that governed the nation.

Just as the Regulators were beginning to shut down courthouses in the summer of 1786, some members of Congress met at Mann's Tavern in Annapolis, Maryland. This gathering was known as the Annapolis Convention and included several of the nation's founders, such as Alexander Hamilton and James Madison. They discussed issues with the Articles of Confederation.

We need a stronger central government to collect taxes and resolve economic issues.

Congress also needs to be able to put down insurrections and keep the radicals in line.

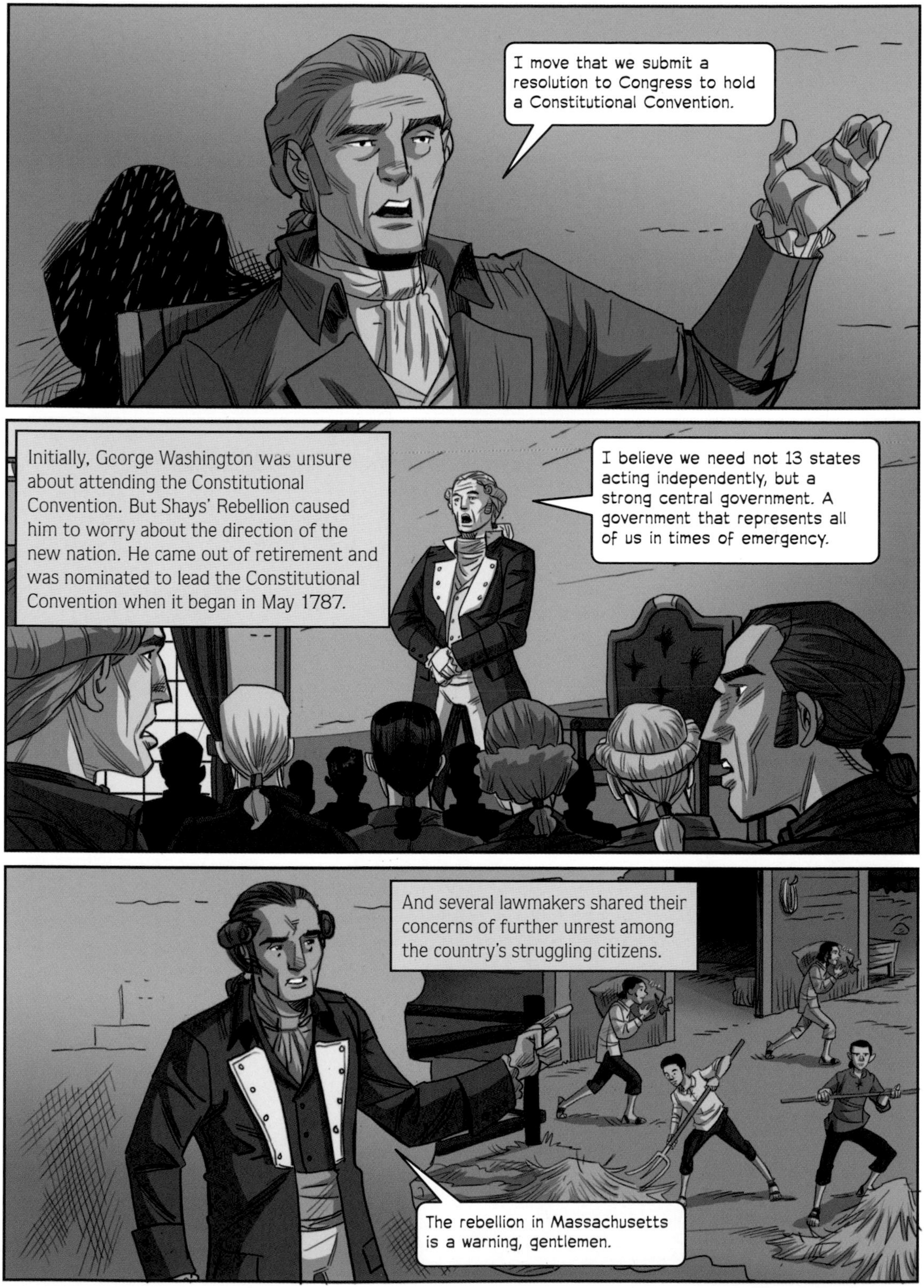
I move that we submit a resolution to Congress to hold a Constitutional Convention.
Initially, George Washington was unsure about attending the Constitutional Convention. But Shays' Rebellion caused him to worry about the direction of the new nation. He came out of retirement and was nominated to lead the Constitutional Convention when it began in May 1787.
I believe we need not 13 states acting independently, but a strong central government. A government that represents all of us in times of emergency.
And several lawmakers shared their concerns of further unrest among the country's struggling citizens.
The rebellion in Massachusetts is a warning, gentlemen.

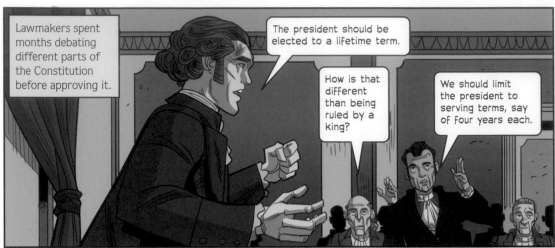

Lawmakers spent months debating different parts of the Constitution before approving it.

The president should be elected to a lifetime term.

How is that different than being ruled by a king?

We should limit the president to serving terms, say of four years each.

Then it was sent to the states to ratify. On June 21, 1788, New Hampshire became the ninth state to approve the Constitution, making it the law of the land.

In April of the following year, George Washington took office as the nation's first president.

Long live George Washington!

Long live the president of the United States!

While Shays' Rebellion was a minor conflict, it greatly affected the history of the United States. The unrest it caused was one reason George Washington came out of retirement to serve as the nation's first president. The rebellion also influenced some important parts of the Constitution.

Article I, Section 8, Clause 1 of the Constitution gave Congress the power to collect taxes. The national government was then able to take on the states' war debts, which helped them economically.

Article I, Section 8, Clause 12 gave the government the ability to form a standing army. The government then had the power to suppress internal conflicts like Shays' Rebellion.

Shays' Rebellion was the last push for a broad, inclusive democracy. While the efforts to include women, the poor, indigenous people, and freed enslaved people would continue . . .

. . . Shays and his supporters sped up the process of replacing the Articles of Confederation with the U.S. Constitution. At more than 230 years and counting, that governing document remains one of the world's oldest active constitutions.

# MORE ABOUT SHAYS' REBELLION

- Daniel Shays was born in 1747 in Hopkinton, Massachusetts. He died on September 29, 1825, in Sparta, New York. He was 78.

- Shays married Abigail Gilbert in 1772. Their first child, Daniel, was born a year later. It is not known exactly how many other children they had.

- Shays fought in some of the most important battles of the Revolutionary War. They included The Battles of Lexington and Concord (1775), The Battle of Bunker Hill (1775), The Battle of Saratoga (1777), and the Battle of Stony Point (1779).

- It is unclear why Shays' name was attached to the rebellion. He was just one its leaders, but Shays was well-respected among the Regulators for his years of military service and his ability to command. He also led the failed attack against the arsenal in Springfield.

- Shays had served in the Continental Army for five years and, like most other soldiers, he eventually received compensation for his unpaid years of service. Shays was given a pension and used the money to buy land in Sparta, New York, where he lived out the final years of his life.

- Pay for privates was about $6 a month, which was a lot for the time. But soldiers had to buy their own uniforms, gear, and weapons.

- Most soldiers enlisted for three years. But after 1788, the majority had a clause in their contracts stating that they had to serve until the end of the war. This was true of the soldiers in the Mutiny of the Pennsylvania Line.

- Congress approved the U.S. Constitution on September 17, 1787. But it then needed to be approved by nine of the 13 states before it would become law. On December 7, 1787, Delaware was the first state to ratify the Constitution. New Hampshire became the ninth state to approve the Constitution on June 21, 1788. The U.S. Constitution officially became the law of the land on March 9, 1789.

- As with the Articles of Confederation, the U.S. Constitution was not perfect. Over the years, 27 amendments have been added to it. These additional laws have furthered the rights of the nation's citizens. Making slavery illegal and giving women the right to vote are just some of the protections these amendments have added to the Constitution.

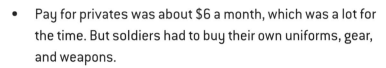

# GLOSSARY

**arsenal** (AR-suh-nuhl)—a storehouse of weapons and ammunition

**colony** (KAH-luh-nee)—a place that is settled by people from another country and is controlled by that country

**constitution** (kahn-stuh-TOO-shuhn)—the written system of laws in a country that state the rights of people and the powers of government

**debt** (DET)—money that a person owes

**democracy** (di-MAH-kruh-see)—a form of government in which the citizens can choose their leaders

**disgruntled** (diss-GRUNT-uhld)—displeased or annoyed

**emissary** (EH-muh-sayr-ee)—an agent or representative of a powerful person

**financial** (fye-NAN-chul)—having to do with money

**grievance** (GREE-vuhnss)—a formal expression of a complaint

**indigenous** (in-DIJ-uh-nuss)—native to a place

**militia** (muh-LISH-uh)—a group of volunteer citizens who are organized to fight, but who are not professional soldiers

**minutemen** (MIN-it-men)—soldiers who could be ready to fight for their country

**negotiate** (ni-GOH-shee-ate)—to bargain or discuss something to come to an agreement

**prosperity** (prahs-PAYR-uh-tee)—doing very well or being a success

# READ MORE

Beckett, Leslie. *The Story of the Constitution: Creating the U.S. Government.* New York: Lucent Press, 2017.

Hoena, Blake. *Fighting for Independence: An Interactive American Revolution Adventure.* North Mankato, MN: Capstone, 2019.

Silva, Sadie. *The Articles of Confederation.* New York: Cavendish Square Publishing, 2022.

# INTERNET SITES

*DK Find Out!—American Revolution*
dkfindout.com/us/history/american-revolution

*History.com—Shays' Rebellion*
history.com/topics/early-us/shays-rebellion

*U.S. History*
ushistory.org

## ABOUT THE AUTHOR

Blake A. Hoena grew up in central Wisconsin, where he wrote stories about robots conquering the moon and trolls lumbering around the woods behind his parents' house. He now lives in Minnesota and enjoys writing about fun things like history, space aliens, and superheroes. Blake has written more than 100 chapter books and dozens of graphic novels for children.

## ABOUT THE ILLUSTRATOR

Passionate comic book artist Eduardo Garcia works from his studio (Red Wolf Studio) in Mexico City with the help of his talented son, Sebastian. He has brought his talent, pencils, and colors to varied projects for many titles and publishers such as Scooby-Doo (DC Comics), Spiderman Family (Marvel), Flash Gordon (Aberdeen), and Speed Racer (IDW).